TRAGICALLY
STRONG

TRAGICALLY STRONG

NAVIGATING THE CHANGE WHEN LIFE TURNS UPSIDE DOWN

PAULA JEAN FERRI

Tragically Strong
Navigating the Change When Life Turns Upside Down
Text Copyright © 2017 by Paula Jean Ferri

paulajeanferri.com

Cover Design by Megan Sawyer
Interior book design by Francine Platt, Eden Graphics, Inc.

ISBN 978-0-9997673-0-6

1. Main Category Non-Fiction—Self-Help
2. Sub Category Non-Fiction—Communication and Social Skills
3. Sub Category Non-Fiction— Motivational and Inspirational

First Edition
10 9 8 7 6 5 4 3 2 1

Printed in the United States of America

Dedicated to my parents,
without whom I would not have been able to
heal from half the traumas of my life.

TABLE OF CONTENTS

INTRODUCTION

Importance of Healing

I'VE HAD A REALLY ROTTEN WEEK. I got yelled at by customers at work, and they weren't just angry, but they were incredibly condescending, like I didn't know how to do my job. Then I had to deal with an ex telling me he suddenly didn't owe anything for back rent he swore he would pay me for. It's just a thousand dollars; no big deal, right? (Please note the sarcasm.) Next, I officially had to purchase a hearing aid, making me feel older than my thirty-one years, and broke to boot. I found out my mom needed surgery, and I was nowhere near home to help during the surgery or the recovery process. I was busy working overtime at my job while trying to write this book and study marketing techniques, so I was also kinda sleep deprived. It was a long week.

Guess what? We all have them. Things get hard, and, at some point or another, life, quite frankly, just sucks. My bad week isn't the point of this book, though. The point is it doesn't always have to be so rotten. I'm generally a fairly happy person. It amazes me how often people are surprised by how happy I am, given some of the things I've been through. Like the time I was homeless, was sexually abused, or had broken off not just one, but two engagements, just to name a few. Not only that, but when terrible things happen, others are surprised by how quickly I can bounce back.

I say "quickly" despite the amount of time it actually takes to figure things out. But I figure you can spend a lot of time focusing on and working on actual healing, or you can spend a lot of time making more of the same mistakes, if not more mistakes, by skirting around the issue. Skirting around things seems like the long road to me. I'll cut right through it, thanks. It's just as hard, but takes a *lot* less time.

There are certainly other ways of moving forward with life. I'm not saying I have all the answers. They are different for everyone. However, this book contains the principles and ideas that helped me when I have hit my lowest points. I've dealt with my share of tragedies. I've struggled through suicidal thoughts when my entire life has come crashing down around me.

When literally everything fell apart, and it felt like life was blocking any kind of good thing for me, not just in one instance, but for *months* at a time, it felt like there was no other option but death. I felt like life didn't even want me, anyway, so what was the point? Life may not have wanted me, but after several months like this in a constant state of depression, seriously questioning whether I should continue or toss myself into the ocean, I realized that even if life didn't want me, I wanted to live.

When everything in life seems stripped away, rather than looking at the shreds of what used to be your life, the goal is to see it as a fresh canvas. You get to start over and build things *better*. Sometimes loss is a benefit. It's an excuse out of the life that you feel trapped in and the opportunity to build and create something better.

If you aren't willing to deal with problems head on, the only other option is avoiding them. Sure, it's easier, but it causes a lot more problems later. For example, what do you do when you break up with a significant other? Again, there are a lot of ways to react, but each choice boils down to either moving through the hurt or avoiding it. How much time do you spend before moving on to the next relationship? (It will be different for everyone, but just for an idea, I average about a year before I get into another relationship. Sometimes it's longer, sometimes it's shorter. It's different even for me.)

Healing is a process, and there are steps that need to be taken. The order isn't important; the timing isn't important. What is important is the healing. It means becoming better for the experience and the things you learn rather than shrinking from the next challenge. Let's work for healthy relationships after getting out of a rotten one. Let's not become hard and cruel just because others have been that way to us.

After a broken relationship, I find I need the time to recenter my life. I don't want an ex to have any influence in a new relationship. The time after a relationship is like a detox. It's a fresh start. The same thing happens after other events too. Time to heal and detox helps you to move forward with a clean slate without hurt hanging around like an old ex.

Let me tell you about my friend Zeke. This friend of mine has been through a lot in his short twenty-something years. He works fourteen-hour days and sometimes is called in to work on his days off, and overtime isn't optional. He has been through several jobs with bosses that can't seem to treat him reasonably well. He is going through a lot of physical pains, including having a major surgery. When I say physical pain, this isn't the small kind. He's had his heart broken too. It came out of the blue, when he had thought things were going well.

Zeke's story breaks my heart. He is generating more debt, his relationships with people are suffering, and he is sacrificing his health far more often than he should. He doesn't even realize it. He tries to get a leg up, yet at the same time, he digs himself a little deeper into his hole. I have watched him grow more angry, pushing away the people closest to him. He already has enough on his plate, and I watch as he continues to make things worse for himself.

Everything that happens to Zeke, from what I understand of his attitude when chatting with him, must be the fault of others. So he gets angry over little things. My wise grandmother told me often that "if it isn't a matter of life and death or a matter of eternal consequence, it's just a minor inconvenience." The little things that bother Zeke cause him to get angry, and he lashes out at others. This, in turn, causes him more troubles in his relationships.

Here's a secret: relationships are central to a happy life. If we can't get along with anyone in our lives, there will only be problems. Problems at home, with a significant other, with friends, at work. My friend places wedges between him and those who care about him most, not to mention those who could actually help him.

The funny thing is, all of Zeke's troubles started with one particular event—a breakup. After being in a serious and committed relationship for years, Zeke's girlfriend walked away and broke his heart. Not only did it break his heart, it broke him. He hasn't recovered. He became a different person, questioning his worth and his ability to make decisions. Even Zeke's physical troubles started after this event. His entire life has hit a downward spiral, and a large part of it is due to not taking the time to heal and figure out where his life is going from here.

That's what we are going to get into in this book. We'll find the steps and questions to help you figure out where to go in the low spots. We'll learn how to move forward, not just with the passage of time, but in actively improving your life rather than just letting it happen. Don't be like Zeke, living in pain and making it worse. Don't ever question your worth or wonder if life's worth living, because it is. It just requires healing.

Time does not heal all wounds. *You* take steps to heal your wounds, though it does take time to do so. The time will pass anyway. I'd rather deal with pain now than run from it for the rest of my life. There's still pain involved either way. I'm not so naive to claim that pain won't be there after you work to heal. However, healing will take you out of the downward spiral and will significantly improve your quality of life.

There may still be pain, but it's not constant. There are moments of peace and happiness. Those usually happen with healing. Who wouldn't want a break? Let's jump in and get you that much-needed respite with some ideas that will help you move forward with that healing.

THE VIEW

Find Another Point of View

YOU KNOW HOW when your friend is having a rough time, and he or she is talking through things with you, everything seems so clear? Of *course* your friend should make this particular decision; why can't they see it? But it's only obvious to you because you have an outside perspective. If you are inside a house of mirrors, it's not so easy to see the way out. If you were above the mirrors and looking down, though, it would be plain to see the path one should follow. Hard times are kind of like this. We just need to see things from a different perspective. Taking a step back and looking at other options helps us in the decision-making process.

Sometimes seeing a different perspective means realizing that things won't be exactly how we want them to be. Sometimes the outcome is different, sometimes the choices we make will have to be different. We have to recognize there is no such thing as perfection or one particular course that will always work.

For example, I am in love with the BBC film version

of *Pride and Prejudice*. From the first time I saw it, I thought it was perfection. I once saw a version that crammed the story into ninety minutes and put a modern spin on the classic tale. I absolutely hated it. It was nothing like the book, and I also thought it was kinda tacky. However, in speaking with my friend Paul, I learned that he had loved that version. This surprised me on many levels. However, he made a point I had never considered. Remember how I hated that this newer adaptation of *Pride and Prejudice* was nothing like the book? And by nothing, I meant it only had the key components?

Paul's favorite part was precisely that the creators of this movie took the story so loosely and made it modern. When watching movies, Paul likes to take into consideration the artists' interpretations. I obviously had not even considered this angle. This idea intrigued me, and I went back to watch the film with new eyes. Confession: it still wasn't my favorite version of the story. However, I didn't vehemently hate it anymore either. Paul's concept made me give a lot more stories a chance than I would have previously. Reading alternate versions of fairy tales is now one of my favorite things.

Paul's view gave me a fresh perspective. Seeing things from his view made me appreciate a lot of stories I might otherwise have avoided. This is a simple example, but it was incredibly eye opening for me. I have benefited not only from the stories I now get to read and enjoy, but also from understanding Paul's alternate perspective. Ironically, his view was in favor of varying outlooks. Every artist has a different interpretation of the same character, same story, etc.

I've come to love seeing how people add their own twists, part of their own souls, into the parts they play in a movie or the words they write on a page. I love how personal tragedies and triumphs can be heard in song covers. I no longer care if something is exactly like the original. The same holds true for people too. We can't all be the same. We are too different and have too many stories of our own to tell. People's differences bring a sense of beauty to my life that I wouldn't be able to find on my own.

Sometimes we need to take that step back and look at things a different way. When life sends a plot twist, we sometimes have to either change our course of action or change the direction we are headed. You can find a new perspective in several ways.

As I mentioned, I love finding different perspectives in reading alternative fairy tales and stories. I've found stories do a great job of mirroring real life—including troubles. I tend to read a story putting myself in the main character's shoes. As I read how they make choices and how they think on their journey, I see things just a little bit differently. I can see varying values used to make decisions. I see how various characters tackle problems, and they work from separate viewpoints than the ones I usually have.

Every person you meet is going to have a different

view of your problem. It can be hard to share; I get that. But wouldn't the fresh view be worth it? Talk to someone. Anyone. Talking it out sometimes can give us that different perspective on its own. If not, you now have a sounding board who can share what they see and give some advice and feedback. That fresh view may be just what you need to start healing.

Validation

Sometimes we need a little validation. It's important to remember that when nothing seems good in the world, we still contain goodness in us. Everyone has strengths. Sometimes it's hard to see it within ourselves, but it's there. In order to really heal, we need to remember that we are worth healing. We have good traits, we do good things, and we have good experiences. Those are the things we need to remember. Not only does it help us move forward, but it helps prevent future hurt, too.

It amazes me sometimes how much we allow ourselves to put up with. I do it too. We allow others to say mean things to us and to hurt us. Take for example your job. Many people hate their jobs. They don't like what they do, they don't like their coworkers, they don't like their boss. It amazes me how many memes there are on the internet about hating Monday, not wanting to go to work, and having the desire to leave. If that desire is so strong, why don't we just leave?

You deserve to like your job. If you are doing everything you can to make it a good environment and still can't manage to have a good day once in awhile, it might be a toxic situation that you should leave. Yet we stay. We stay for the paycheck, as if we couldn't get that from another, better occupation. We do it for the insurance benefits or the 401K. It's not worth it.

At one point in my life, whenever anything bad happened, I swept it under the rug. It was fine. "I can keep going; no big deal," I thought. "Things could be worse. I have no reason to let if affect me like this." I couldn't even validate my own feelings. I was ignoring my own feelings as if they didn't matter. As if *I* didn't matter. I matter, so why wouldn't the way I felt make a difference? I numbed myself to feeling the bad things. Problem is, that made me numb to the good things as well. You can't pick up one end of a stick without picking up the other end.

Our feelings and emotions are part of us. Emotions contain a power in them. The stronger the emotion, the stronger the action that might come from it. The angrier you are, the more likely you are to act on it. The happier you are, same thing. Think of that power contained within us. Imagine what we are capable of if we stop fighting ourselves and instead use those emotions in an effective and positive way. Direct that energy somewhere. Don't cover it up. You have to allow yourself to feel those emotions, because if you try to fight them, you will eventually lose. Fighting against yourself isn't the best way to use all that energy. Let yourself feel sad, lonely, angry, etc. Let me restate this concept: *There is no right or wrong way to feel.* It's how you act upon those emotions that leads you toward positive outcomes or downward spirals.

How you feel about an experience is just as natural as the color of your eyes. Just let it happen, but don't let it consume you. Feel it and acknowledge it. However, remember that it is a feeling, and feelings can change. The circumstances that led to the feeling won't change. They're in the past. Letting yourself feel sad will not bring back an ex or a loved one who has passed. Anger won't get your job back. Whatever the event that has already happened, it won't change. Memories are powerful things. That emotion you felt in the moment will always come up when you are looking back on it.

When you allow yourself to feel emotions rather than telling yourself "I shouldn't be angry" or saying "I'm over it" when you're really not, you acknowledge the validity of your feelings. It's ironic to me how often people seek validation from anywhere and everywhere—except the most important source. While getting validation from others is incredibly helpful, the most important validation you can get is from yourself. Let yourself hurt, get angry, feel happy. There is nothing wrong with feeling emotions, even if they don't seem to fit a particular situation. Validate yourself, and you are finally able to start moving forward.

In order to truly heal, we need to have validation. For both ourselves as a person and for the things we feel. Without it, when healing gets hard, it's easy to just give up. Don't give up. You have already survived so much; don't let it go to waste. Once you recognize that you are of infinite value, and that what you feel and think are worthy of respect, you've taken an important step toward becoming whole (and the word *whole* is a possible origin of the word *healing* from Old English).

LABELS

ONE WAY WE DERAIL the healing process is through our tendency to put labels on ourselves and on others, defining who we are and who they are. We hear these phrases all the time: "I am so dumb," "they are black," "they are white," "he is gay," "she is racist." Insert any other adjective we use today. These labels are meant to help us understand who we are and who others around us are. Problem is, our labels can be very, very off. The good news is you get to choose which labels you listen to and which you don't. There are two sides to this coin.

Some problems come from this habit of labeling others. For example, there are people who don't fit the mold. Just because someone is part of a group doesn't mean they are identical to every other member of that group. No matter the similarities at the group level, each person is unique once you get down to the individual level. You may be a senior in high school, just like several others, but you may be the only one with Tourette syndrome. You may be a corporate executive, but the only woman in your company with that role. It can even be as simple as being in a band, but being the only one in it who plays the saxophone.

The point, again, is that you may have things in common with a group, but you can still be different. Sharing one trait doesn't mean you share them all. Take, for example, this line from the movie *Sweet Home Alabama* said by actor Josh Lucas: "Darlin', just 'cause I talk slow doesn't mean I'm stupid." How often do we assume one thing leads to another? We have to be careful, because when we assume something about a person based on a category they're in or a label they have, it can actually lead us to make racist, sexist, or other other similar kinds of stereotypical observations. Yes, labels can help us understand large quantities of people. Just don't attach values to these labels and assume things about who people are and how they make decisions. For example, people from Japan are Japanese. This label doesn't necessarily carry any value in itself, but simply describes a fact. And if we know anything about Japanese culture, we can understand a little more about people with the label "Japanese." Dealing with one person, though, does not require the use of labels. This person may be an outlier to a general label that is given to a large group of people. While a person may have been raised in Japan, they may also have American parents and live a blend of the two cultures. Get to know them, just like you want someone to get to know you, rather than assuming you know their life story or that they know yours.

When we jump to conclusions about people based on a group they're a part of, embarrassing or offensive situations can follow. I once watched a video in which an educated African American woman was told, "You speak really well." As opposed to what? As an educated individual, why wouldn't she talk well? Just because some others with the same skin tone don't? She didn't speak any differently from the person who made the comment. Her backstory was assumed, and it appeared to the other person that she had a struggle she had overcome. See how assumptions based on labels can grate on more than a few nerves?

The ironic thing is how we are so quick to shun some labels and so quick to attach ourselves to others. I love to connect with others who give themselves the same labels I give myself and who share the qualities and interests that I have. For example, some of my personal labels are that I am a writer. I am a woman. I have Tourette syndrome. I am Italian, Mexican, French, Swedish, Scottish, British, German, and Native American. I am . . . what am I? *Who* am I? These are labels I attach myself to and love. Some labels I choose. I love writing and I choose to spend my time doing it. Some labels I don't like. I don't enjoy being called an airhead when my memory falls short or a klutz for not being able to walk in a straight line sometimes. . I am, however, proud of the fact that I can work to improve my memory and gracefulness, and the awkward charm that comes with them in the meantime. I can still accept that these labels aren't wrong, embrace them and use them to my advantage.

Labels can give us a sense of belonging. They allow us to see commonalities and make connections that we normally wouldn't have. Have you ever searched your favorite things on Facebook? There are groups centered on anything you can imagine. I am part of Facebook groups connecting me to people who went to the same high school and college; groups from plays I have been in; groups for authors; groups for Tourette syndrome; groups for church; groups for shopping LuLaRoe (help me, I have a problem); groups for entrepreneurs; groups to advertise free Kindle books (these are awesome!); groups centered on health and wellness, finances, or dancing; groups in memoriam of friends who have passed; a group for yard sales in my hometown; groups for podcasts I follow; and several others. I'm not even in a small portion of groups you can find online, and more are created every day.

Even with those people that share the same label as me, there are still differences in understanding. Just because I consider myself a writer because I write, someone else might not consider me a writer unless I actually publish. I consider myself a fan of *Harry Potter*, but someone else might not consider me a fan unless I am a full-extreme Potterhead. I like *Harry Potter* books, but I have only read the books once and watched all the movies once. I'm not even in any Facebook groups for *Harry Potter*.

So how do you know which labels are right for you? That depends entirely on you. *You* are the one who makes the decision about the things you like and don't like or what you believe and don't believe. I actually took time when I was in my early twenties to sit down and make a list of who I am (including who I want to be and traits I want to develop). I highly recommend this activity. I learned a lot about different ways that others may perceive me, and it was this exercise that helped me realize my talent of being a chameleon.

I have a long list of roles I fill, all very different and diverse. Even looking at jobs I have had, I see that I have a very wide skill set. Here are just a few of the jobs and occupations I have engaged in over the years:

- a page in a public library
- an RA for college apartments
- a cleaning lady
- a grocery bagger and cart pusher
- a sandwich maker
- a deli/bakery worker
- a cashier in a pharmacy
- a voice teacher
- a caregiver to a young man with cerebral palsy
- a tutor
- a salesman
- a secretary in a mortuary

- a violinist at a public event
- a network marketer in the jewelry industry, financial world, and health industry
- a recruiter and a customer service rep for a call center
- a self-published writer

Noticing all these roles that I have filled (and that is just in the professional world; I didn't include family roles and church roles I fill), I wanted to write them all down as a reminder of which roles are the most important to me. I chose the labels that define me. I know who I am and where I want to go. Choose your labels wisely. Understand that they can change. This has helped me make so many decisions in my life and has given me a sense of direction, which has been central to my healing.

Giving Direction

The labels I have chosen give me identity and direction. But labels vary in their very definition from person to person. So we can't really depend on labels given by anyone else, because they change when applied to a new person with a completely different background and experience. In order to fully understand who we are, we have to set our own definitions of these labels and then figure out which ones fit us the best.

If I depended on labels given to me from other

people, I don't think I would be able to recognize myself. In fact, I did this for many years. As a child, my world revolved around books. What I most wanted to do was read, and I did a lot of writing in between. As I grew older, I started to listen to others saying that it wasn't normal to spend so much time lost in the pages of a book. As a result of putting other people's opinions ahead of what felt right and natural to me, I started to get involved in other things and ended up being pulled in many different directions.

I went through several different majors and then spent quite a while in the workforce after college before I stopped listening to those other voices and decided to do my own thing. Before I continue, though, I do need to mention the following. Many of the labels attached to me by others were accurate. As I said in the introduction to this book, sometimes we need outside perspective to see things about ourselves that we may not realize. For example, I never would have thought I was a good singer if I hadn't been told by others and encouraged to explore this possibility in my life.

Part of the reason I am now so sure about myself and what I do is the incredible amount of time I've spent doing other things. I found a lot of really wonderful things that I do enjoy more than I thought I would. It is up to me to decide if I want to use a particular skill as a career, make it a side hobby, or drop it complete-ly from my life. Let's go back to the singing example. I sang along with the radio, generally without really thinking about it. I was told I had a nice voice and that I should try out for choir for my sophomore year of high school. To my surprise, I made it. I fell in love with music, and my first college major was in music.

But my very first semester in college, I had a professor tell me I would never graduate as a music major, that I didn't have the talent. My stubbornness came out, and I did get my associate's degree in music, mostly to prove him wrong. However, I then took a break to serve for a year and a half for my church. I discovered I liked working with people and wanted a career involving people more than music.

This led me to the degree I graduated with—International Cultural Studies with an emphasis in Communications. During my final year of college, I was faced with a decision. In order to graduate I needed to either find an internship or write a senior research paper. I still had no idea what I wanted to do career-wise, so I chose the research paper. I was warned by several people that I would not be able to find a good job out of college if I didn't choose the internship.

Here's the funny thing: again, others were right. I graduated and had to take entry-level positions with little chance for growth in the company I worked for. The beautiful thing is how my life came full circle. That college paper I wrote? It became my first published book. A career as an author was where I needed to be. Without all these false starts and setbacks, I might not have the willpower now to make my current career work. Careers are hard. You have to love what you do and work really hard for it. So while the labels were my biggest setback in getting off to a quick start in my life's plan, they are also what will help me find success.

This might sound like I'm cherry picking. I am—and it's okay! Sometimes I listen to others. Sometimes I don't. I choose what I want in my life. I can let someone's words hurt me and hold me back, or I can choose not to listen to their negativity. I can let their compliments and encouragement propel me forward. I can also shy away from the nice things that are said.

Notice the phrases in the previous paragraph that start with "I can." In the Spanish language, verbs are treated differently than they are in English. Getting to know the Spanish verb for *to can* was an incredible experience for me. *Poder* means "to can" (as in "I can do this," but based on Spanish grammar, this is a generic term for the action), but it can also be translated as *power*—the power "to can," or to be able to do. You have the power to act on any "I can" statement you choose. You also have to power to choose not to. It is your will, your choice, and your power that make that decision to follow through. It's more than just ability; it's a choice and an action.

Power of Choice

My favorite thing about having a choice is that it allows for great flexibility. Things don't have to be one way. I don't have to listen to *everything* people say. I also don't have to completely *stop* listening to others and what they say. I don't have to ignore compliments. I don't have to listen to cutting remarks. I choose. Because I can. I have that power to choose. I can totally understand why people get power hungry; it's a terrifyingly wonderful feeling to realize that power you have when you exercise your ability to choose.

What gives us this power is the inability for the negative to hurt us. We are not defined by the things that happen to us, but how we respond to them. Acknowledging our faults and knowing they are there makes such a difference, but we don't need to let them bring us down. Vironika Tugaleva once said, "Let yourself face your demons. Love them, but don't believe them. Then, you will not need to let go. They will get up and leave."

Have you ever had a sibling or a friend pick on you just to see your reaction? The more you get riled up, the more they revel in pushing your buttons. Soon you are all riled up. If you've ever stopped reacting to their teasing, it's amazing how fast they get bored and stop. The same principle happens with negative traits. Knowing what they are gives them less sting. Viewing them with calm acceptance instead of allowing them to drive your actions gives you the upper hand to use them to your advantage.

Some of the best wisdom I have ever received is that advice is just that—advice. It works for some and it doesn't for others. *You* are the one who determines if it is good or bad advice. Approach it with an open mind. Be willing to try. If it doesn't work, stop. Just stop. It may sound like good advice. It may even work well for a lot of people. That doesn't always mean it will work for you. Sometimes advice can lead you to take a good trait to the extreme.

This was a hard lesson for me to learn. I love people, sometimes to a fault. I am always giving people the benefit of the doubt, trying to see things from their point of view, arguing in their favor despite pain they repeatedly cause me. Often I would keep them in my life because I loved them. I was loving them so much, I didn't see the harm they were causing me. It took me many years to learn I could still love them, but they didn't have to be right by my side, and they didn't have a right to take advantage of me. In fact, I can love a lot more when I allow more people into my life, as long as I remember to take time for myself and to love myself, too. It is a good thing to love others, but it was important for me to remember to love myself.

I struggled to find a balance between self-love and love of others. While I lean toward the side of loving others, another person may lean towards the side of self-love. If we are trying to find a center of balance in our lives, good advice for one person might be completely opposite for another. I may need to be reminded to love myself more, and Sally might need to be reminded to share more with others. I'm not saying Sally is a bad person. She has traits I need, in fact.

Have you ever heard the phrase "opposites attract"? Sally and I are different, but she might remind me to pay more attention to myself, which I need, and her reminders and reaching out to me are good practice for her to think of others. We could potentially be each other's best reminders and make each other better people. A word of caution, though: just like everything else, this could potentially go the opposite direction. If I'm so busy taking care of Sally and Sally isn't thinking of me at all but taking advantage of me, we end up bringing out the worst in each other.

Again, it comes down to your choice. You choose if you keep Sally in your life. Is she helping you? Are you helping her? Once you figure that out, you get to decide. You choose if you listen to the labels she gives you. You decide if she gives you good or bad advice. Once you make a choice and then see the difference it makes, it becomes easier to use this powerful tool as you continue to grow in confidence and acceptance— of yourself and those around you.

Differences Make the Difference

Another benefit of labels is that they make you different. We are conditioned our entire lives to believe that difference is to be avoided. We sometimes ostracize those who look, talk, or think differently from what is considered the norm. But difference is actually a good thing. Differences are what give you color on a blank canvas. Each label is a color, creating the masterpiece that is you.

You may share some colors with others, but no one is going to have the exact same picture on their canvas.

I used to view my differences as negative qualities. As sad as that sounds, all I could see was what was wrong about me. I (thanks to my Tourette syndrome) was disruptive and noisy. I was stubborn. I was shy. I read too much. Get my drift? But this is where things get exciting. I came to realize that these qualities I saw as defects were actually my gifts.

My Tourette syndrome has been a larger blessing than a curse (as I mentioned in my book *Awkwardly Strong*). While I may be stubborn, I know how to use that stubbornness to get things done, and I work hard for the things that I want. It's also known as tenacity. As for being shy, I didn't talk to people very often growing up, but as a result, I did an awful lot of people watching. Guess what? That's almost a requirement to be a writer. You have to understand human nature and how people interact. I did a lot of that since I didn't dare actually talk to anyone. My reading so much helped me to understand stories, and creating stories is how I want to make my living.

These supposedly awful things that I hated about myself when I was younger have become my greatest strengths. Nothing really changed except for how I view those traits. Changing how I look at them allowed me to see the true potential I really have. It helped me to love and appreciate who I am and, more important-ly, love what I do and feel a purpose and passion every day that wasn't there before. Who knew my "bad" traits could make me so happy?

The cool thing is that once you reach this epiphany, it expands with positive effects in other areas of your life. When you have this understanding of yourself, you suddenly gain confidence. That's infectious. People suddenly want to know what changed. You are suddenly sought out. You get to help others change for the better. It starts small, like all good things do. You influence those closest to you—your friends, your family, your coworkers.

For example, when you create your personal culture and the labels you give yourself, you then get to help create and influence the interactions with your family. Your family culture has the capability to change. You will influence rather than control your family members, for others still create their personal culture and make choices accordingly. Influence is far more powerful than control, though. When you influence someone, allowing them to keep their own control, you are not constantly involved in a power struggle. When you influence positively, people begin to trust you and follow suggestions. This doesn't always happen, but it's not like we can be right all the time, either.

How do we create this influence? When we see ourselves in a different light, we begin to see others in a different way as well. The more we practice seeing good in ourselves, it gets easier to see good in others and all around us. However, it is also possible that it can have the opposite effect. Sometimes as we see ourselves growing more confident and powerful, we tend to see less of others, because we are too busy looking at ourselves. This can lead to wanting more power and more control and a sense that those around you "aren't worthy" (even though they totally are). I've been fortunate in that I've always had a tendency to see the good in other people. That had both pros and cons. When I was younger, I compared myself to those around me. The problem wasn't that I admired their good traits. It was that I was blind to my own strengths. This false comparison was part of the reason I thought I was so terrible at doing things for so long. Listening to that mental critic can be hazardous to your self-esteem.

It wasn't until I learned to judge in a fair and balanced way that things changed for me. It meant understanding that I had immense value to bring to the world, and so does everyone who has ever lived. Itt meant learning to see that we all have strengths and we all have weaknesses. It also meant being honest about both my strengths and weaknesses. I had to acknowledge and be grateful for my abilities and at the same time acknowledge my weak points and seek to turn them into strengths. And I had to do the same with others. I had to learn to recognize good traits, and then learn how even bad traits can become helpful and powerful, and I began to see the amazing potential in every person I met. And as I did so, I came to recognize the same truths about myself.

To illustrate, I am an introverted person, but the loud and "annoying" extroverts that I meet help bring me out of my shell. They are good at talking to people and can help others feel at ease when they use their abilities positively rather than letting them take over. Our differing abilities can be our greatest strengths.

So don't compare your weaknesses to others' strengths, or vice versa. See the differences between you and others and find the good things in each of you. See how you can help others. See how they can help you. No one person can do everything. We have to be different in order to work together. Never forget that the things that make you different give you an advantage, especially if you know how to use the traits that other people hide because they haven't learned to look past the negative side of those traits and see the possibilities instead.

NOT THE END

Moving Forward

One key thing to remember is that when absolutely rotten things happen—and they can happen often—it's not the end of the story. Your life continues to move forward. The good news is that so far, you have a 100 percent survival rate. You can survive. The real question is this: are you going to keep up with that ever-changing life, enjoying and flourishing as you go? Life isn't about a single point in time, good or bad. Your life has more happening than just this single event. Life is more than a rape. Life is more than a funeral for a loved one. Life is more than a beating.

On the flip side, life is more than one good moment too. Don't wait and live for a promotion, thinking that when you get it, then you'll be happy. Things don't magically get better with a fairytale wedding. Life is a compilation of moments, and you choose how most of them are spent. Will you spend life reliving the past or figuring out how to heal, cope, and improve the future? There is more to your story.

When I was living in Hawaii, I went on several hikes. One hike was to Laie Falls with some friends. We hiked in quickly, trying to make sure we had plenty of sunlight so we could spend some time there and make it back before dark. Upon arriving at our destination, it was not what we had anticipated. Laie Falls is unlike many of the falls that we had previously hiked. Those came complete with large amounts of water cascading over cliffs and collecting in a large pool for swimming. This was more like a trickle down the side of a hill, and it wasn't deep enough to really swim in. We were slightly disappointed, but that quickly changed once we started back.

We slowed down now that we weren't rushed to get to the end. The disappointment did not last long, as we finally started to notice what was around us the whole hike. The views were simply stunning! I think we had more fun on the way down pointing out particularly gorgeous cloud formations, phenomenal flowers, and fabulous views overlooking the North Shore. The nice thing about the return journey is you get to see what you missed on the way in. Too bad time doesn't work quite the same way—we never get to travel back. But we can take what we've learned from the past and apply it to our ongoing journey.

Had we only paid attention to that particular moment when we saw the falls, it would have been a big waste of time and a disappointing hike. Luckily, the story didn't end there. It may have been the end of the hike in, but it was not the end of the journey, since we then had to hike out. After we made it down, we went for food. It was still not the end of the day. There were more moments to be had, and there are many more to come in your life too. Keep pushing forward.

The Bigger Picture

Realizing that life is made of many moments strung together to make up a large number of days, weeks, months, and years that are continually changing helps us take a step back and realize that what we are dealing with is just temporary. Life changes on a constant basis. We tend to look at just what is right in front of us in the here and now. We don't look at what got us to this point. We don't look at how it will affect the future. We don't look at how it affects others around us as well. Zooming out until we can see this bigger picture allows us to make better decisions that affect and improve our future instead of being mired in the problem of the moment, endlessly spinning our wheels, unable to escape from the muck.

Sometimes it's really hard to tell how things are going to affect us in the long run. Looking that far forward from where we are at, we can't always see what's coming. So instead, I also try to take a look backward. What in my life has led me to this point? Am I going against everything I was ever taught? Will that take me the direction I want to go? Am I living according to the morals I hold most important? Am I improving?

You will notice these questions don't point toward specific events. Each of these questions are directed toward our own ethics. This code of beliefs will vary by person. You have to figure out what is most important to you. There is no right or wrong answer. If you were forced to choose between honesty and intelligence, which would you choose? Both are good and important things. What about any other virtues? There are patience, love, optimism, justice, equality, gentleness, moderation, passion, kindness, gratitude, loyalty, beauty, cleanliness, respect, honor, and more. If you could only choose one, which would it be? How do you want to be known? Which of these are you known for now? How would your friends and family describe you?

These principles and virtues have been around longer than you have. They will be here long after you are gone. It won't matter what country you lived in, the language you spoke, the school you went to, or the type of car you drove (if you even had a car at all). These virtues can be found anywhere and are highly sought after and valued. Why would you not want to aspire to become something so precious? Looking at these values and virtues, no matter which one(s) I choose to look at, I feel both small and awed, filled with a greater sense of purpose. I see a bigger picture. Something more than just me. The bigger picture is not a timeline. It is our values and how we live our lives.

As all encompassing as these principles are, what makes them so penetrating is the little moments. Those moments when no one else is around to see. Those times when "it doesn't matter" actually does matter. A lot. It's what you do or say when someone cuts you off on your morning commute. It's your response when someone flips you off. It's how you handle hearing lies and rumours spread about you. These are the moments you see what principles people attach themselves to. This is the bigger picture. What are you choosing?

When you make important choices, do you recognize yourself? Are these the choices you want to be making? Is this how you want to be remembered? Because trust me, your choices will be remembered by the people they affected. It's hard to think of such things when in the heat of the moment. It's easy to become angry, even if you want to be temperate. It's easy to get upset when you want to be optimistic. Values are hard to live, which is what makes them hard to acquire and so preciously worthwhile.

How well do you know yourself and the values you stand for? Whether you know it or not, you are daily projecting the principles you stand for. What message are you sending to the world? No, this is not a Facebook quiz. I really want to know. What are the top three most important things in the world to you? For me, the three most important things (in no particular order) are my relationship with God, my relationships with my family, and living in such a way that I am able to experience joy. I've worked really hard in each of these areas, but they were not always a strong suit for me.

That didn't prevent me from recognizing how important these values were to me. I've taken the time to figure out what works and what doesn't and how to improve in these areas. Without these three things in my life, I simply wouldn't be me. These three things affect so many of my decisions that I make on a daily basis. Those who know me know that these are important to me, sometimes because of conversations we have, but other times because they can see it reflected in my decisions.

What do your decisions say about you and what is important to you? Do they match with what you just said were the most important values in your life? They don't always line up. I had to figure out how my values were affected by seemingly small decisions. We've all had that happen before. We make a seemingly small decision, like going to see a movie, and then we learn after that there were things we didn't realize going on during the movie. Maybe it was a movie that didn't align with your moral principles. Maybe your mom tried to call and you ignored the call because you were in the movie and it turned out to be important. It's good to keep improving as you work to align your behavior with your values.

One of my favorite stories has always been *Beauty and the Beast*. I love various tellings and different spins. I recently saw the musical in a local theater, with my friend Erica playing Belle. It was right after I had published my first book, and I had just finished reading it on my Kindle. It was fascinating to watch the play through the lens of my book's message of being true to yourself, quirks and all. The play echoes the themes in my book. For example, Belle is different from everyone else in her village. The Beast is not your typical prince either.

I was fascinated with a line Belle says and the way she brings out the idea that the Beast made a wrong decision, and she even calls him a fool for thinking his decision was okay. Both characters make decisions throughout the performance that lead to the ultimate conclusion of the story. Belle makes decisions based on her love for her father, while the Beast's decisions change as he learns how to make his choices match the values he wants to hold. As the play progresses, the Beast's stupid decision becomes the vehicle for making Belle's thirst for adventure and fairy tales come true. Was it really such a wrong decision after all? Maybe it was, maybe it wasn't. People are going to have different views. It will depend on the lens through which you view the event. What is the primary focus of your moral compass?

The Beast's character progression in many versions of this story is wonderful. His cruelty and heartless decisions lead to his exterior matching who he is on the inside. He is transformed into the monster he acts like. At the beginning of the story he is unable to recognize the things he wants. He can see only hopelessness and pain. As he grows to value kindness and friendship, he has to alter the choices he makes in order to match those values. His growth and change lead to the ultimate happy ending.

The Beast's initial decision to imprison Belle's father and his offer to trade him for her freedom may not have had the best motives behind them, but Belle and the Beast eventually both choose to make the best of the situation. They both learn to adapt and grow. Had the Beast not made the decision to keep Belle's father prisoner, the entire story would have been different. Growth is never easy. Sticking to values that are important is not easy. Changing what we value, what we find important, as the Beast did, is also incredibly difficult.

I absolutely loved this idea that even bad decisions can have a good outcome. Just because I make a mistake doesn't mean I fail. How encouraging to know that sometimes our "stupid" mistakes lead us to the greatest victory. This is something that was continuously holding me back as I was growing up. I was always afraid to make a wrong decision. I had to go to the "right" school (nope—had to transfer), pick the "right" major (I went through three of those), and date the "right" guy (let's just not even go there). I obviously chose poorly many times over, and I wouldn't have it any other way.

Even with all of these "wrong" decisions, like the Beast I still had the ability to change. Growth and learning and change are not only possible, but also necessary. In other versions of this story, it is the beauty who makes significant changes, allowing her to move past her initial fear and/or prejudices in order to understand the kindness of the misfigured "beast," who is simply different or misshapen, though kindhearted.

Even when we make wrong choices, the point is, it isn't over. We can change and make things better. Even when it is a big deal and a significant change, we can learn to see things differently.Going back, the Beast might not have made the same choice, but it still led to his salvation. Had he not imprisoned her father, he would not have met Belle and his curse would not have been broken.

Though we make wrong choices, it's not the end of the world. We can always improve ourselves and make something good out of the original bad. We can learn from the wrong we did. It doesn't make the wrong thing right, but the miracle is that the wrong thing can lead to a blessing in our lives and others' lives if we learn the right lessons from it.

With any kind of change, we must first reassess values and understand how we make our decisions. While I may say that joy is important to me, sometimes I don't realize that there are things taking away from that. I have had relationships in which I was convinced I was happy. Once these relationships ended, I realized how much better off I was. Sometimes we see things the most clearly looking back. I had thought the relationships were so important, and ending them was miserable. Putting a few years between me and the experiences, though, makes it more clear how silly I was.

This is a pattern that happens multiple times in our lives. When we allow ourselves to heal correctly from difficult instances, we can look back and see the benefits and progression more than the pain. I'm only going to touch on this lightly, as healing looks different for many people. However, during the rough times in our lives, we sometimes have to extend the pain. We can't just push it to the side or ignore it. Yes, it hurts more, but the only true path to healing comes from dealing directly with the pain. Otherwise, it is like a wound that you don't clean out because it hurts too much, only to have it become dangerously infected. I would rather have a year of pain now than several years of skirting around an issue, causing more pain in myself as well as in others. Healing comes back to this idea of seeing the bigger picture.

At this point, we get to look at what our values do to our decision process. The principles we espouse, at first glance, can sometimes stand in the way of the things we want. However, one of my favorite quotes, despite being from an unknown author, is "Don't give up what you want most for what you want now." When we make decisions based on what we want now, we can't obtain the happiness we all seek.

For example, say it's payday. You have some money left over after paying bills. What do you do with it? This is a decision that is based on your values and that bigger picture we keep talking about. First option: You go shopping. You get that new dress, a new pair of shoes, a new game, the newest phone on the market. Maybe you even buy gifts for other people. Giving is important, right? Second option: You save for a bigger purchase. You can take a large vacation, buy a home, or pay for college instead of taking out loans. Third option: You invest or save for retirement. Which option do you choose?

Remember to focus on the things that last beyond the moment. If you only focus on the now rather than looking down the road, you purchase instant gratification by sacrificing things of greater worth. You sacrifice good health for the price of that soda or supersized meal. You sacrifice financial freedom for the brand name. You sacrifice the chance of true love for no-strings-attached physical attraction. The values and priorities you set are evident in every moment, and they tie the moments together in a bigger picture. Seeing this bigger picture allows you to take control of the moment as it passes. It's not just the past, just the present, or just the future. It's how they all tie together.

Positive and Negatives

Taking a step back allows us to see the good and the bad right next to each other. I really like being able to do this, because sometimes the bad doesn't seem so bad when viewed from a distance. That step back gives you a different perspective. As rotten as some days can be, the next day things might look different. If nothing else, I know what *not* to do again or what I would do differently to make a similar situation better.

I tend to be a very optimistic person, and I'm also slightly competitive. So I gave myself a challenge, compliments of the movie *Pollyanna*, and tried to find some good in rotten news. Today I found out that the trip to Paris I had planned wasn't going to pan out. A connecting flight was canceled and the airline couldn't find an alternative, so they refunded my tickets. I have been planning this trip for several months. It was going to be my first trip out of the country, and I had invested a lot of time and money into this trip already. I was simply livid. (Note that although I tend to be optimistic, I am human. I reserve my right to flip out when things don't go my way.)

At the same time, taking a step back helped me remember that I had just quit my job to write full time. The extra money from all the refunds and being able to use the money I had saved for the trip might actually not be such a bad idea. While this incident might not compare to a really serious problem (life-threatening illness, being in a terror attack, losing a loved one), the lesson is valid regardless. And every time the lesson is reinforced, it gets easier to handle life's problems with equanimity. For example, I wouldn't go back and choose to be homeless again, but the things I learned during that time make me a more compassionate person. This is something I strive to be. There are so many good things around us all the time, even in the hard things, but we don't always see them.

I'm still fairly young, but I have already learned that sometimes it can take years for us to really find a purpose in our struggles. Problems that I dealt with as a child or a teenager didn't become understandable to me overnight, but with time, experience, and hindsight, I have come to see meanings in my struggles that weren't obvious in an earlier season. For instance, I suffered from depression and suicidal thoughts for years, starting in my teens. I struggled with understanding who I was and what purpose I had. Who knew that the years it took me to figure out who I am would later allow me to help others. Now that I'm in my thirties, I find myself referencing that difficult time of my life often. Because I have experienced that pain, I have greater empathy and can relate with sensitivity to those who are still fighting their battles.

Not only have I been able to help friends navigate through similar phases in their lives, but I've found immense joy in realizing that I can do this as a lifestyle. How ironic is it that my stress over who I am and my temporary inability to find a purpose in life is what actually *gave* me a purpose? I am not the only one who has experienced this. The trials we face, after years of healing, often become the launch pad for the rest of our lives.

So why do we look at everything through a negative filter? Why do we only see the *cannot* and not the *can*? Why do we see someone with Down syndrome and assume they will never be a model? Or a fashionista?

Why do we assume someone with Tourette syndrome could never be an actor? Why do we assume someone who does things differently could never be anything other than a burden? Why do we assume we are too old, too fat, too skinny, too tall, too short . . . too anything?

Take, for example, Maysoon Zayid. She is a comedienne and actress who is breaking barriers left and right. Not only does she have the stigmas following her of being a Muslim and a woman, but she also deals with cerebral palsy. She could have several reasons to have low expectations for life and what she is capable of. Yet she has overcome every label and negative comment thrown her way. She didn't see what she couldn't do; she saw what she could do, even if she had to prove it to others.

There are negatives in this world. I understand this concept very well. There are different opinions. There is no pancake so thin it has only one side. There are ups and downs and difficulties. However, what I'm saying is that in the long run, if we ignore the bigger picture, we hold ourselves and others back from our true potential. That can sound really harsh, but hear me out. Holding yourself back does not affect just you. There are others around you, watching you, learning from you. What are you teaching them?

Sometimes I get so frustrated when I witness the amount of stinking thinking humans love to wallow in. We all have our bad days. We are allowed to spend time being angry, sad, and so forth. Just don't live there. Just as you are allowed to feel down, you are also allowed to feel happy, joyful, excited, and ecstatic. It doesn't matter what it is that makes you excited. If it's dyeing your hair purple, then for heaven's sake, dye your hair purple! I don't care what excuses you have and what you think is holding you back. Chances are, it's most likely made up or unimportant.

Granted, there are exceptions. There is a code of ethics that crosses cultures, languages, and religions. Things like, you know, not killing people, not taking something that doesn't belong to you, and the like. It's not hard to be kind to others. Focus on being kind, and most everything else will follow suit, falling into place.

There are also limitations. Do not confuse them with exceptions. Someone who is confined to a wheelchair has a limitation, not an exception. They have limited use of their body, but they still have an active mind. They are still capable of doing so much, sometimes in an unconventional way when it comes to most things physical. It may not be your definition of "normal," but it is normal for them. They still have a life to live. They have thoughts, feelings, and emotions to communicate. They are still people, even if they do things differently.

Here is another thing: You shouldn't be nice to people because they deserve it. You should be nice to people because they are human. They also have their bad days and good days. Just because your interaction with someone isn't a positive one doesn't mean you need to continue that cycle. Just because you didn't see them bring dinner to a struggling neighbor—you only saw them cut you off in traffic—doesn't mean they don't deserve a touch of kindness. In all honesty, can you say you deserve kindness in return for your actions 100 percent of the time? No one does. That doesn't mean we shouldn't be kind to each other.

We should always give kindness, at least as often as we are able. When we aren't up to the task, that's when we allow others to give kindness to us, meaning we also have to be willing to accept it. We have to be willing to see the kindness in others. Sometimes that means we have to get help. I was raised to be incredibly independent. Accepting help was not only hard, but I actually hated it. I didn't want to depend on anyone. One day I realized that just because I accept help once in a while and let others give kindness, it doesn't mean that I depend on it. I am still independent, but I'm much more willing to allow others a part in my life by being kind. Turns out, those are the people I want in my life anyway. I want to be around others who are willing to be kind and share goodness in the world rather than those who aren't.

Interesting how we sometimes push away the people who are trying to help and somehow stick around the ones that would bring us down and increase the negativity in our lives. That's not to say that they aren't good people with dreams and good intentions like the rest of us. However, why wouldn't we want to expand our circles to include those who like to do good things, who have a great attitude, who look for the silver lining in every cloud. Just being around people like that is contagious. They leave us feeling happy and hopeful. We should be around people who inspire us, who push and stretch us to do more good and to be better.

The more I find these types of people in my life, the more I hear others saying this about me. People say that I'm good and inspiring. I'll be perfectly honest: it still surprises me. I just like to see people happy. I like to be happy. I'm kind of saddened by how rare that type of positive example seems to be—especially if I am the one others find inspiring. On the other hand, that should boost your confidence. I'm not too different from anyone else. I am still human, after all. If I can do it, why can't you? Don't go there. You can. Turn those "can't" phrases into "cans."

The thing to remember is you aren't any different from anyone else out there who is living a happy, successful, and balanced life. You have strengths like they do. They struggle like you do. But in all of the self-help books and articles I've read, the most common thing mentioned is that we need to see the big picture. Look at a collection of moments, and don't get stuck in just one. How does what happened in the past help you going forward? Remember that sometimes it can take years to see the reason behind events, but don't stop looking. Like all skills in life, you'll get better at it with time and practice.

Struggles

You will struggle in your life. We all do. But it's the struggle that makes the end result all the more amazing. Those that overcome great difficulty are the ones that see the most success. Overcoming hardships is what gives us our strength. Staying within our comfort zones not only doesn't allow for growth, but it doesn't allow for success. It makes us . . . average. Isn't it ironic that those with the most to gain from their differences often strive to simply be normal?

This prompts the question: does being called "disabled" actually make a person "more-abled"? I have never been a fan of the word *disabled*. Everyone could be called disabled in some way. No one is perfect at everything, and everyone will have struggles. Everyone also has strengths that give them more capability in something than others. I am not disabled. I am "differently-abled." The main thing to remember is that you are capable. You touch lives and inspire others.

There are people who are less physically capable than others. They can still become cheerleaders or swimmers. Some might prefer to become artists or musicians. Maybe they write books. They are capable.

There are people who don't communicate the same way most people do. They still have thoughts and feelings. The more time you spend with them, the more you understand what they want to say. Maybe the way they communicate is through art or music. Maybe they prefer to become an athlete, like a boxer or a soccer player, and express themselves through movement rather than words. They are capable.

What about you? What holds you back? Are you clumsy, but long to be a ballerina? Maybe because you are clumsy, you prefer to study, read, and write. Who says you can't be a blind dancer? Who says you can't be a deaf musician? This is a challenge. Prove the naysayers wrong. It's a hard road, it's true. However, those that travel it are in good company. Beethoven was a deaf composer. One of the best. He could have given up when he lost his hearing. Instead he chose to find ways to make it work. He would place pianos on the ground so he could feel the vibrations through the floor. He improvised, and his music is still played almost two centuries after his death.

So really—who says what you can or can't do? Let's take it one step further. What do *you* say about your abilities? Really, that's the only opinion that matters. I was a bookworm as a child. My parents got a little worried about me and grounded me from books for an entire summer. I was so enveloped by stories in my mind that I started to write a few. I decided I wanted to be a writer.

Here is where I don't want you to misunderstand. I love my parents, and I love the way they raised me. I'm grateful for the life I've led, influenced and guided by their choices. But sometimes I wonder what life would have been like had I continued writing at a young age.

My parents never discouraged me from writing, but they very much did encourage me to go to college and get a stable job. As time went on, I drifted away from writing.

What could I have done had I continued on that path back then? I'll never know. Some may call this tragic. Here's the thing: I don't know that I would really have much to write about if I hadn't gone out and experienced life first. In the process I discovered so much more about myself and the world around me, which in turn made me a better writer. It taught me new ways of looking at ideas. It taught me to think outside the box. It gave me courage to try new styles and genres. I still write fiction (and have plenty of exciting ideas just waiting to be put to paper), but my first published book was nonfiction. Not only did writing this book help change my style of writing, but it allowed me to gain a deeper understanding of myself and the world around me. It also allowed me to meet and connect with others who have the same dream of becoming a writer as I learned and studied about the publishing process.

Knowing others who are in the same boat as I am is so validating, especially when it gets hard:

"It's not long enough."

"I suck at words."

"Does this even make sense to anyone but me?"

These common writing fears are familiar to anyone who has ever tried to write. I've been lucky to find great encouragement and support in the writing community. Maybe it's because the other writers have all experienced the same fears and doubts that they are so generous with their advice. I have learned so much from them, and my writing is better for it.

The struggles I face as a writer also allow me to connect with others. For several people I know, their struggles are now strengths that have given them a profitable business. A famous example, though he's not a friend of mine, is Dave Pelzer. As a result of his tragic childhood, he wrote *A Child Called "It,"* and he now spends his life advocating for children who deal with abuse and who are in the foster care system. He has played a large role in promoting awareness and putting laws into effect to protect children so they don't have to suffer as he did. Without the struggles, where would he be? How many people would miss out on his help? Hard things are life changing. Depending on how we react to our trials, we'll come out on the other side for the better or for the worse. Let the struggle make you strong.

Allow Yourself to Hurt

Hurting is an important part of the healing process. We can't heal if we ignore how much we hurt. Not only does acknowledging our pain start the healing process, but it also allows us to remain soft, rather than becoming hardened and jaded. Wait, don't tune me out just yet! Being soft is actually an important characteristic. Being soft does not mean being weak. It's the balancing of softness and strength that is so difficult. It is possible to be both soft and strong. Over 2500 years ago, the Chinese philosopher Lao Tzu said, "Water is the softest thing, yet it can penetrate mountains and earth. This shows clearly the principle of softness overcoming hardness."

Remaining soft tends to be the last thing we want. Being soft and open means we are going to get hurt again, doesn't it? Luckily, no, it doesn't have to. When I was ten years old, my parents were devastated to learn that they would never get to meet their unborn son due to a miscarriage. However, just because my parents lost a child, it didn't mean they could never have another, or that they couldn't enjoy the three they already had. Just because every romantic relationship I've been in so far has ended, it doesn't mean it will always happen that way. We can choose to be soft hearted and open to positive experiences yet to come. As we grow and change, we become more suited to the state we desire. We grow and change based on what we want to become. If we want to be successful, we read books about our chosen field, we make investments, we start projects, we make mistakes, and we learn from them until we reach the status of "successful." We do the same thing with any state of being. It doesn't matter if we want to be happy, successful, popular, or even alone. Henry David Thoreau once stated, "Things do not change; we change."

My parents taught me how to hurt through their example. They let themselves hurt when they lost

Garrett, my brother. It still hurts. However, that hurt has also turned into compassion. They know how it feels to lose a baby. They have been a strength to others who have had the same experience. I have watched them care for others many times over, not just for those who have lost a child, but for those who experience various kinds of grief. My parents know what heartbreak feels like, no matter the individual situation. In each case, not only have they blessed the lives of others, but they have created an opportunity to remember their son and honor his memory. His short life has made a lifetime of difference to my parents and to those they touch.

My parents can't change the fact that Garrett passed away. However, they changed as a result. The awesome part about tragedies is ironically also the hard part: they create a space for change and growth. They allow us to make a choice: the choice to become bitter or better.

Now making that decision is pretty easy. Who doesn't want to be a better version of themselves? It's the acting on this desire that is hard. It's difficult enough to not be dragged around by the hard times life throws at you. It's easy to get upset at those trying to cheer us up, because they don't understand our pain. So inadvertently, and on occasion maybe even intentionally, we hurt others around us. Like the old adage "Misery loves company" tells us, we feel less alone when others have a taste of the pain we feel.

While you're going through misery, this line of thinking can feel justified. All it really does, though, is create more pain, not only for everyone else, but for you as well. It's an endless cycle and incredibly destructive. As it was stated in *Fiddler on the Roof*:

Villager: An eye for an eye and a tooth for a tooth!

Tevye: Very good. That way the whole world will be blind and toothless.

Thankfully, life isn't fair. We often don't deserve the bad things that come our way, but goodness also exists in this world and also comes our way on occasion, even if we don't deserve it. The thing is, we have to realize we don't deserve it in order to really appreciate the goodness that comes our way.

Without pain, we would never know there was a problem, and we would not heal correctly. If you didn't feel pain when you had broken your arm, you wouldn't take the necessary steps to recover, and you would only be causing more problems down the line. Pain allows us to heal and to determine how we want to heal. Will it make us softer and more aware of others, or will it make us hardened and bitter? This is the most important choice you can make in the midst of your struggles.

LITTLE THINGS

It's the details that we find through long, slow, meticulous study that help lead us to greater understanding and from there allow us to change the world. It's always the small and simple things that make the biggest impact. If you want a big fire, you are going to need a lot of wood. But the biggest heap of wood does nothing until lit by a small match. Have you ever tried to eat a meal without any kind of seasoning? Just a pinch of salt can completely change a meal.

With that knowledge, never let a small difference keep you from moving mountains. You are meant to be different. You are meant to be the salt on a meal and the spark that creates a bonfire. Being different is a gift. It adds spice and variety to life that would be rather dull without you in it. This gift is what not only makes you *you*, but what shapes and inspires others around you. You have something that no one else has. Do you disagree? I used to think there was nothing special about me. I felt common and invisible. For heaven's sake, even my name is so common I have to publish under a pen name (okay—I didn't have to, but it did make marketing easier).

Not only are these little differences in you so key to the world, but so are the choices that you make. Take, for example, procrastination. Everyone does it. We all have ways to put off doing important things we know should get done. Most writers can attest that right up until the deadline when they really have to stay glued to their work, they can be found cleaning the house, checking their email/social media, or "doing research," which includes getting sucked into the internet down a wormhole of random information that ends up being irrelevant.

Staying focused is a small decision, but it's very hard to follow through with. As we discussed before, it's the small choices that we make every day that will eventually lead us to where we want to be. If we make that small choice to do other things before sitting down and actually writing, will the book ever be written? No, it won't. Which is a shame, because the world needs your story. It needs your voice and your little differences.

It's the little things that can make a big difference. One small bullet can end a life. One short phone call can bring earth-shattering news. No matter what pain you are in, one small moment got you to where you are today, did it not? The reverse also holds true. It's those little choices that we make day by day to move forward and to heal that will get us back on our feet. Bruce Barton, an author and politician in the early 1900s, once said, "Sometimes when I consider what tremendous consequences come from little things, I am tempted to think there are no little things." Don't sweep things aside because they are small. Small habits, baby steps, tiny details—all are the single steps that lead to great outcomes.

Choices

When something affects you, especially deeply, you have a choice. Choices are hard. There is always going to be an easy answer, but that is almost always the wrong one. My grandpa passed away during my senior year of high school. We were close when I was younger, but as I got older, he got more and more sick and slipped away from us day by day. Just because I miss my grandpa doesn't mean I should be angry at the world. Just because I have had broken engagements doesn't mean I'm always the victim. Those would have been easy decisions to act on. Yes, bad things happen. I accept this as a part of my life, and then I move on to the next experience. Each and every emotion I feel makes up a part of who I am.

Every experience we have and the choices we make, or don't make, continue to affect us. It's just like a bamboo plant. When the plant is young, it can be shaped into various designs. Google "bamboo shapes" and you'll see. They can be hearts, spirals, and other intricate patterns. Bamboo doesn't shape as well as it matures, though. We as people are the same. The older we get, the harder it is for us to change shape. The sooner we understand this process, the better. Although, thank goodness, we can make life-altering decisions our entire lives. We just tend to be creatures of habit, and it becomes harder to change those set patterns. So we have to be careful not to let ourselves get into a rut of negativity as we get older.

From the time we are young, the things we experience teach us how to go forward. We are taught along the way by those around us. The closer we are to them, the more influence they have. Their stories and backgrounds guide us as we learn to process the goings-on around us. We start creating habits at a young age. Again, they are changeable, but it's more difficult to change as we get older, so we have to be vigilant! When something good happens, do we go out to celebrate? Or do we let it quietly happen with no fanfare? How about picking out the flaws in ourselves or others? The longer we practice an action, the harder it becomes to change. How about when we make a mistake and vow to do better and be better next time? Do we really make that vow stick, or do we put it off for another day when push comes to shove?

Our choices are as limitless as the events we experience themselves. What about when bad things happen? How do we respond? Do we choose not to choose, simply reacting with whatever is easiest? Do we choose to actively be bitter? Do we ignore the bad thing because it's just another notch in a long line of many? Do we see how it can help us long term? What about helping others in the midst of your pain? *You* decide what you want your life to look like. Others may try to advise you, but that doesn't mean you have to listen.

I am amazed at how often I witness people feeling bad about something that makes me absolutely joyful. In case you didn't already know, I have Tourette syndrome, and it happens to be my favorite thing. I don't want you to say "I'm sorry" after I tell you I have it. I'm not sorry at all. People try to bring sorrow into a situation where none exists. People will do the same thing with any emotion—bringing anger, fear, disgust, and even joy to situations. You don't have to feel the same way they do. You are the one who makes the choice of how to react, of how something affects your life going forward.

Action vs. Reaction

One of the most important choices we will make is what role we will take in our own healing. We need to be proactive and take control of this process. Taking action allows us to heal correctly (remember becoming better, not bitter?) and even sets us up for happiness once we have gone through this healing process. I'm not saying you have to heal completely on your own, but you are in the driver's seat. You determine what needs to be done and what is best. When we are able to acknowledge and accept whatever tragic event we experience, we are able to determine the next steps to move forward.

The best people I know are the ones that expect nothing but do a lot. They understand that life is cruel and difficult, yet still they smile. They help others. Lifting others and doing good is second nature to them, and they don't even think twice about it. They almost seem surprised when someone is willing to reciprocate and help them out. Bad things happen, but that doesn't take away their ability to choose how they'll act.

I say "act" for a reason. I don't want you to simply react to what happens to you. I mean, it is your choice, but passive reacting takes away that ability to choose, doesn't it? Someone cuts you off in traffic, and the natural reaction is to get mad, right? Where does that take us? (Hint: we've been over this part already.) You then cut off someone else, who then runs a red light because you slowed them down, and this natural reaction thing can keep going on and on.

Take control of the situation! Don't let the anger take control, resulting in a more aggressive driver. You can get angry without acting on it. Or, rather than getting mad, we have a myriad of other emotions that we can choose to feel. We can feel confused, sad, afraid, or surprised. Maybe you even decide to ignore what happened and continue on your happy way. *You* decide. Decide to take control of your life! Then keep doing it. Practice makes perfect, after all. Don't just react. Take control and make a choice.

Once you take control, acting instead of reacting, you get so many things in return. Not only are you taking control of your life, but you are also empowering yourself to do and be good. You become the person others aspire to be. Power and goodness . . . those are certainly things I want. I want the ability to take control of my own life.

For so much of my life, I simply reacted. I was always willing to let others do what they wanted, and I didn't have the self-confidence to say otherwise, whether it hurt me or not. I let myself be miserable, because I thought it was all I deserved. Turns out I was very wrong.

The worst summer of my life happened while I was away at college. My boyfriend and I broke up, all my friends had gone home for the summer, and I slowly lost everything that I had based any kind of worth on. I lost hours at work and was barely making enough to pay rent. I was able to buy maybe a little food, but not much. The newly ended relationship had not been a healthy one, so on top of breaking it off, I was trying to figure out what had happened and how to cope in the aftermath.

On top of that, I had just been told I couldn't be placed in an internship because of my Tourette syndrome, which forced me to choose a completely new career path. I wondered if I was even in the right place, or if I should just move home. I felt discarded and worthless thanks to the professors who told me I couldn't continue in this path I had envisioned for my life. I thought my entire future had just been taken away from me.

With my friends all home for the summer, I had no one to speak with and vent to in order to figure things out. So I became a bit of a recluse. I went to work every day, though I was only allowed to work five hours per day. The rest of the time was spent in my room—usually in my journal trying to figure my life out.

Then came the day I was told at work that not only could they not give me more hours (never mind I was barely working enough to survive), but they might even have to let me go. Now I had zero job security, so I could be unemployed at any moment. So I started trying to save and stretch my already thin budget tighter. There weren't many other job options in this little town that I could turn to. I wasn't eating well. I was stressed beyond anything I had ever felt before. I was unable to sleep at nights. If I took a sleeping pill, I could *maybe* get four hours of sleep per night.

Bad sleep and bad eating started to take its toll, and I started getting sick. While I still went to my job every day (I couldn't give them an excuse to get rid of me just yet, and I needed every penny I could earn), my life was slowly deteriorating. I had already lost so many things.

Now, just a bit of backstory here: I have always been a religious person, and my relationship with God has always been my first priority. However, during this time of my life, when I felt like I needed Him most, I felt abandoned and alone. And I got angry. I questioned whether He even existed.

I hit my lowest point when I realized that in questioning with such anger, I had lost my faith. My faith had always been my defining characteristic, and now I had lost myself. I didn't even know who I was anymore, much less what to do with my life. What do you do when you have gone so far you don't know up from down?

Part of me is ashamed to admit (though part of me is glad I can relate to others in the same situation) that I sought ways to end my life. Every time I thought it couldn't get any worse, it did. I had no hope, no refuge. My family was thousands of miles away, my faith was gone, my career plans were in shambles, my love life was nonexistent, and there was nothing even remotely promising around the corner. As I sat in my room, literally right across the street from the ocean, listening to the crashing of the waves, I wanted nothing more than to toss myself into the mercy of the sea. However, even that required more energy and effort than I had at the time.

I was merely existing as an empty shell. I still consider it to be the worst time of my life. Where do you go from here, when you get so low you don't even have the energy to commit suicide? Let me tell you what I was doing. I would wake up and go through the motions of reading my scriptures and praying out of habit. I then watched a Japanese anime until it was time to go to work. After work, I would call my mom on the walk home. With such distance between us, there wasn't much she could do besides lend a listening ear. Following that I would watch more anime until I would try to fall asleep for an hour. After failing to sleep, I would wake up and journal until I actually could sleep, only to wake and repeat the cycle the next day.

Lucky for me, the anime I was watching ended up saving my life. Who would have thought? Of all things, a cartoon in a language I didn't understand changed my life. At one point in the story, one character in a rebel group turned herself in to save her comrades. As they came to save her, she kept telling them to stop. Leave. Save themselves, because she wasn't worth saving. Oh how true those words echoed in my soul!

Then the rebel group told her to forget about being saved and instead asked if she wanted to live. She thought about it for a moment or two. The story flashed back to scenes of when she joined the group, to fun and happy times they had shared before her capture. She then fell to her knees, crying through her tears, "I want to live." She was, of course, then rescued.

In all honesty, I have never watched another episode of this show. I stopped it right there, in tears, and pulled out my journal. I decided I did want to live. I just had to learn how. I also realized that no one was going to save me. I had to figure this out on my own. I would have a lot to learn and a lot to fix, but I wanted to be happy again. It took several months of hard work. I stopped reacting. I started doing. I had a purpose now. My purpose was to figure out how to be happy. And once I had it figured out, I needed to take the steps necessary to really feel it.

I continued my frantic journaling, analyzing every aspect of my life. I found another major to study and a new direction in life. I forced myself to go out with friends when they returned for school, giving me a release every once in a while. I made new friends. I refocused on my prayers and reading the scriptures, rather than just going through the motions.

It was a long road, but one day in September (which is now my favorite month), I was walking home from my classes. I had found a new major to study, stayed in Hawaii, and found a new place to live that was not so haunted. My old friends came back, I had made new friends, I rediscovered my relationship with God, and I realized . . . I felt it. I was happy. Why? I survived. Everything else was simply icing on the cake.

I was incredibly happy with my new major (holy validation Batman!) and happy to no longer feel alone, and I realized how lucky I was to be where I was and in my new apartment. However, everything simply paled in comparison to this feat of surviving. I did it. Not everyone does. I can totally see why. No judgment here. However, I was so grateful. I had come so very far. I found myself again. I still have rough times and continue to feel pain. But I have moments of pure euphoria too. Beyond happy. Beyond joy. I experience moments that cannot get any better, and I feel perfection in where I am with my life.

I had to be the one to realize that I needed to make changes in my life. While I couldn't always control the outcome, I was still able to be more proactive, rather than a spectator of my own life. I made choices that helped me move forward. I did get a lot of help along the way, friends who lent a listening ear, pulled me out of the house when I started to regress, and offered insights I hadn't even considered. But no one could make the choices for me and no one could follow through on those choices except for me.

Commit

Make a commitment. Decide your priorities. Then move forward! That part is simple. It's the following through part that gets difficult. However, following through doesn't need to be a deal breaker. It's just making the same decision over and over. And like everything in life, it gets easier each time you do it. If you make a decision to work out everyday before work, you have to make this decision again every morning. Monday morning, you have to decide to wake up and work out. Tuesday morning, you have to decide to wake up and work out. It never ends; you make that decision every day.

Having to make the same decision more than once does also tend to make us question ourselves. Did I really make the right decision? Is this a sign from the universe telling me I chose wrong? I just don't want to today; I'll start again tomorrow. While only you can ultimately tell whether you made the right decision or not, tough times will come, and you will face this decision again and again to test your level of commitment. How committed are you? Are you committed enough to keep going? Or do you let the negatives win?

Self-doubt, insecurities, fear, and anxiety are all forms of negatives. They don't just come from others. The most dangerous ones are usually the ones found within us. As said by Goi Nasu, "An entire sea of water can't sink a ship unless it gets inside the ship. Similarly, the negativity of the world can't put you down unless you allow it to get inside you." When negatives take root within you, they become hard to pull out.

The hard part about making a decision is really and truly believing that it is possible to follow through and accomplish this goal. What is so hard about believing, especially in ourselves? I'm fairly certain it comes down to the fact that belief takes trust. Oh snap, that just changed things! We can't blame others for our problems and failures?

What does it mean to trust ourselves? Let me explain. I've seen this as a big issue when I make decisions, and I can see it as a big issue for others as well. For example, I can make a decision that I am going to lose weight. I can invest in programs and pay for a gym membership. I've done this numerous times. Every time I do well for a month or two, fail, then give it a year before starting again. I'm starting to realize it's my own fault. I may be the one making the decision and saying I will do this, but I'm also the one that isn't committing to doing this with my whole self. I'm never "all in" with this decision. I've made it before. I've failed before. I want the results without the work. I don't trust myself to put in that effort. I know I won't. But I want to. Not only that, I'm scared that if I do actually put in the effort, I won't get the results that I want. I'm scared that it won't fix everything (and I know it won't. It won't fix my dating life, it won't make me more likeable, etc). It's overwhelming what it won't do. I may not be directly looking at all these things, but they are real and present just the same. So why bother? I don't trust myself enough to follow through and I don't trust the process. Then nothing changes and I'm still stuck in the same rut. This is so subtle I couldn't even see it at first. It took a lot to get me to really see what the core issues were. So now that I know how to get the results that I want, I'm scared to actually make the decision.

On the other hand, it's much easier to know why we don't trust other people. People are fallible. I can guarantee that everyone at some point in their lives has been let down. Someone left you stranded after school because they forgot to pick you up. A significant other has broken your heart. Your best friend told lies behind your back. There are so many more instances that I could name. Some are accidental. Some intentional. All hurt and have broken our trust. It's hard to go through that time and time again. Because sadly, it does happen, time and time again. In fact, I can name times when I have accidentally broken the trust of another person. I can't even trust myself not to hurt others!

So how can we trust ourselves and others? We are humans. No matter how hard we try, we are not perfect. We can work on becoming more so. Some even get close, at least in a few aspects of their life. Mother Theresa was just about perfectly kind and giving and humble. But would she have been able to fix a computer? Probably not. Even she wasn't perfect, although she got really close on a lot of really important things. I'm also pretty sure it didn't happen overnight. She had a lifetime of hard work and hard decisions that brought her closer and closer to that point.

And as a caveat, if Mother Theresa wanted to fix a computer, she totally could have learned. There are classes and tutorials and books for anything you could want to do. We are all capable of learning new things, no matter any kind of difference or excuse you think is holding you back. It may take longer, but it is always possible. All it really takes is making a decision and a commitment to follow through. Decisions are always possible, and you are capable of anything you put your mind to.

Follow Through

How to follow through is one of the biggest things I learned from going to college. Finishing large projects and being around wonderful people doing large and cool things in their lives, even if it wasn't writing a book, was inspiring to me. Are you willing to study? Learn what it takes? Work hard? Push through the challenges? All it really takes is commitment and following through.

Maybe that's what is lacking in today's society. We often lack the passion and the commitment. We fall at the first sign of possible failure—not even actual failure! We settle for good enough. We take the path of least resistance. We give in to peer pressure. It's easier than taking a stand. It's easier than saying "no." It's easier than disagreeing and having fights and conflict. However, conflict is actually a form of growth. Again, it's hard. Yet it's worth it. Might I suggest a better course of action? Make a decision and stick with it. Be careful when you say yes. You should say yes, don't get me wrong. However, there will also have to be a few "no"s to keep you from getting distracted. Don't say yes to so many things that the big things fall by the wayside.

I do this very thing every time I go to publish a book. I get so caught up in different courses and exercises about how to market and how to set up a business . . . and then I do absolutely no writing on my actual book. Which is actually the purpose behind figuring out how to run a business and sell my books. I lose the purpose and main focus for what I'm doing. Then I burn out. Don't do this! Pick something and follow through with it.

This is actually just as simple as it sounds. You don't even need the help of experts, because *you* are the expert on you. When you make a choice, you know your own weaknesses and strengths and what is holding you back. You set a plan that works best for you. Just like with my weight-loss journey, I know I'm the only thing holding myself back. I have the gym membership and the grocery shopping list with healthy foods . . . it's just that it comes time to eat and I *really* want that cookie my coworker bought for me. I'm going to eat it anyway. And I know I'm going to be tired when I get home from work and won't want to go anywhere—least of all the gym. If I'm really going to make the decision to get in shape, I simply have to follow through with what I already planned. Say no to the freaking cookie. Don't go home, go right to the gym, or, better yet, get myself out of bed at a decent hour to do it before work. Nike had it right: "Just do it."

Then be proud, not only of the positive change you've made in your life, but of the self-control you have, which is an incredibly rare trait. That alone will take you further in life than just about any other trait you could develop.

As a caveat, please understand that something like addiction is a completely different animal, and professional help is needed to overcome it. There are some great programs already in place. Here the decision is simply to seek those out and follow the steps outlined. It will still take a lot of self-control, but you'll need extra assistance, so don't underestimate a serious addiction.

It's not enough just to make a decision. I can decide to do anything I want to do. But it won't happen unless I'm taking the steps to make that choice a reality. We can make a choice to start healing, but it doesn't do much good unless we follow through to the end. Half healing isn't much different from not healing at all. It may be a step in the right direction, but not the same as healing itself.

SERVICE

Others

For TRUE HEALING TO HAPPEN, we can't be focused just on ourselves and our pain. This sounds like it's going against most things I've said so far, but this needs special attention. Part of true healing is to not perpetuate the pain that we have felt. An equally important part is helping others to navigate their own pain. Everyone around you has their own pain. Once you truly understand this, not just in a detached, intellectual way, but in a visceral sense, where you come to see all people as an extension of yourself, you will have discovered a powerful tool in the healing process. By turning your focus away from your own pain and troubles, and instead turning outward to become aware of other people's pain and looking for ways to help them up and out of their trials, you will find your own problems shrinking.

If you take this radically effective action, you are quickly going to realize that everyone is fighting a hard battle, as the old saying goes. And when you have that lightbulb moment, you will move from being the victim of your own problems to being a hero for another person.

There are so many ways that you can help. You can reach out with true empathy. You can make sure that your words and actions don't add to someone's hurt. You can help someone else see the good things in him- or herself. You can help someone see there is something to look forward to in his or her life.

I have learned from my parents to take the hard things and use them to my advantage in this area. I know what it feels like to not have a purpose. I know what it's like to feel worthless and not deserving of anyone else's time. So I can now use this in my day-to-day life. I know to look for the good in others and help them see their value.

Just because I see the good in others doesn't mean they see themselves this way. It's kind of sad how often people are surprised by a simple genuine compliment. People would much rather hear the good things you have to say than the bad things. Bring them up. Talk about how awesome your sister is. I mean, you are in the same gene pool. You didn't get *all* the greatness. I'm sure your brother got some too. Not to mention your parents. Yeah, I went there. You have awesome parents. Where do you think I got my tenacity? From my stubbornly awesome parents. They are people too, after all.

It boils down to kindness and respect. That is what gains influence. Think about what Tuesday night would look like, coming home from a long and stressful day at work. The house is a disaster and your roommates are having a few friends over. Do you join in? Or rant about the mess? Maybe it's your children who made the mess. The same question applies. Do you drop your struggles to play with them or yell about the mess and let it add to your stress? Even social media could make it worse if you let it. Social media can be a distraction from cleaning up, or make you feel worse comparing it to Amy's perfect house.

Let's turn it around now. What about how you let your family/roommate/boss/coworkers treat you? Do they treat you with the respect you deserve? Once again, this is where influence is going to have a better effect than trying to control them. Take a step back. They might be picking on you, poking you repeatedly, trying to get you to absolutely explode. There's a fascinating thing I have learned: sometimes people just want to see your reaction, what you will do. They then mirror your reaction. Your explosion allows them to let out anger or hurt they might have been holding in, and you give them permission to be mean to you.

I'm not promising this is why they are doing things. This is a maybe. People are different. The motivation may vary, but there is always a reason. Find out what that is. Easier said than done, I know. I would irritate my siblings in a way that allowed me to feel justified in my actions and self-righteous about how I treated them, but I was treated terribly in return. Truth is, I was just as horrible. I would intentionally ignore them when they tried to get my attention, thinking what I was doing was more important. This would anger them, and as young as they were, they would try harder to get my attention. It would escalate to the point that I ran to my mother, hoping she would punish them. I knew they were young and just wanted attention, and I withheld it from them intentionally, to the point that on occasion, they were the ones who got in trouble.

My self-righteous indignation allowed me to be angry, which I normally would not have allowed myself to be. Anger was a bad emotion, and I wasn't allowed to be angry—or so I had thought. It justified me in how I treated my siblings, or again, so I thought. But I was oh so wrong. I'm still mending those relationships as a result.

The point is, there is never an excuse to be rude. There are rude people in the world, so it may seem only fair to treat them the same way. However, the Golden Rule doesn't say, "Treat others the way they treat you." It says to treat others the way you want to be treated. I can't think of many who really want to be treated on a constant basis like they have no worth. They may believe that about themselves, but that doesn't mean they really are worthless. More importantly, it doesn't mean that they should be treated as such.

You will be amazed at what happens when you treat others as if they are people of great worth and potential, because that same sentiment always comes back to you.

You might be tempted to think that the Golden Rule is so old-fashioned. But it is a true law of the universe, no matter what you call it. It works. You get what you send out. You reap what you sow. And when you sow kind thoughts, giving people the benefit of the doubt, and when you perform kind actions, helping others with their own problems, sooner or later the universe always sends the same sentiments, actions, and help your way.

What You Can't See

We all face tragedy in our lives, and just because we don't see it on the outside, that doesn't mean it isn't there. What you think you know about that happy-go-lucky neighbor isn't always the case. Just because they always have a smile on their face, it doesn't mean nothing is wrong. They may have recently lost their job. Maybe they found out their significant other cheated on them. It's possible a child was recently diagnosed with a life-threatening disease. Perhaps their sibling has just landed a life sentence for crimes committed.

There is a chance that they really are just that happy. But do you really know? It is really easy to think we can tell so much about a person from what is on the surface. One of my favorite things about people is the depth within each of them. There is so much more than what is on the surface. Not only that, but they are all so different. It's impossible to get bored with the millions of collective experiences that people have had, and in such a short amount of time.

The best thing about all of these stories from so many people is learning what worked and what didn't. I have a friend—I'll call her Olivia—who has had her share of bad relationships. When I speak with her, especially regarding relationships, it is now a constant flow of man bashing and her determination to live alone. While I can appreciate Olivia's determination to live alone and the peace that gives her, I have a hard time listening to the man bashing. I know there are good men in the world. I have several of them in my life. A place of resentment is not where I want to be, despite my own consistently failing pursuit of romance and a family of my own.

So what do I need to do differently? I have to be continually open to new relationships in my life. I can't expect every relationship to turn out the same. Sure, most of them will. However, one day, it will be different. I have to be willing to try new things, though. Blind dates, online dating, getting out of my house and being social once in a while . . . and I always have to remember that each person I encounter is different, with their own triumphs and tragedies. I can't assume they are all the same, because they aren't. Again, I have had relationships, and they all ended quite badly. But the good news is that I'm a better person and have a better idea of who I am and what I need in a relationship as a result of the bad experiences.

This same principle also applies to other areas of our lives when dealing with tragedies. When my parents had a stillborn baby, I was about ten years old. I watched how hard this experience was for them, and I've seen how hard it still is for them. I certainly didn't understand. I was only ten, and it's not like I had ever met the baby, so I didn't get it. But I still watched. I watched my parents have a funeral and bury Garrett. My dad continues to decorate his headstone for every holiday, just as he has for the past twenty years or so. I watch my mom counseling other women with this same tragedy, and I see the wisdom and support she is able to give. Most important, I watched our family become a little bit more important to each other and we started spending more time together.

Again, I was once told to treat everyone like they are facing the biggest trial of their lives. Chances are good you will be right, and they will appreciate the kindness and thoughtfulness. Maybe they aren't struggling. There are good moments to be had in life too. Either way, it's those thoughtful things you do to help others that gets them through rough times and gives them strength in the good times to pass it along. The world needs more goodness, and it's going to start with you.

OVERCOMING THE
IMPOSSIBLE

THE COMBINATION of all the principles we've discussed in this book allows us to do things that we
and others may have thought impossible. Sometimes
the "tragedy" in our lives is something that we are born
with that others see as a problem, mostly because they
don't have to deal with it on a daily basis. Tourette syndrome is not a tragedy for me, because I love it and
know how to use it to help me meet people and make
friends, etc. Someone else who has gone their whole
life without it probably doesn't understand. It's different, so they think anyone doing great things is a big
deal, even if it isn't. Why wouldn't someone be able to
achieve their dream? No matter the obstacles, people
do great things all the time. Not just most people, but
anyone, no matter the differences they have.

Take, for example, my new friend Isabella. I watched
a video about her on Facebook and absolutely loved her
strength at tearing down the labels around what she is
capable of doing. I asked if I could share her story and
some of the obstacles she has overcome. Isabella was

born in Guatemala and is a growing name in the fashion industry. She has overcome people fighting against her, thinking she couldn't do what she loves and in such a short span of time. The following is her story, edited for clarity:

When I was born, it meant a big change for my family. I was born with Down syndrome. That moment started what my mother tells me was our journey into the wonderful world of Down syndrome.

I am the youngest of four. [My older siblings are] Alexandra, Christine, and Carlos Enrique.

When I was five months [old] I had a heart operation. They fixed a ductus arterioso, [which is] a little hole in the pulmonary artery. The operation was a success.

When I was two years [old] and I started to walk, I started to go to a regular school, and I graduated from high school al seventeen.

As a part of the requirements to graduate, I had to prepare what they call "My Life Project," and I started to dream go to college to study fashion design.

My mother tells me that I could spend hours watching [looking at] magazines, [and] later I used paper and pencil to trace the figures, and then my mother used to buy me pieces of cloth and I cut and made dresses using only pins for my sixteen rag dolls.

As the rest of my friends, I had dreams to go to college to study, but the colleges didn't accept me, because I have Down syndrome.

I felt so sad. It hurt me just to think I was not going to be able to make my dream come true. But you know what? After a few weeks, I decided I was going to learn to use my sewing machine and to educate myself, so my mother found this academy where I go twice a week to learn how to cut cloth and make clothes, and all of my peers there really love me and help me.

After I started with my sewing classes, my aunt invited me to participate in a fashion event called Guatextraordinaria, where I brought beautiful bags I had made using beautiful textiles. They sold in minutes! So I thought . . . why not start my own line of clothing?

I didn't know my grandmother used to be a very famous fashion designer and had an atelier (studio) thirty-four years ago. It was called Xjabelle, but when her little daughter was killed in a car accident, she closed it and forgot about it . . . until my mother told me. I wanted to make something for my grandma, so I named my brand DOWN TO XJABELLE—Down because I have Down syndrome, and Xjabelle because of my granny's atelier.

In February 2016 I was invited to participate in the Fashion Week in London, and I designed for that big event four beautiful worry dolls. Worry dolls are little straw dolls (one inch long), and the indigenous people say that if you tell the worry doll your problem and put it under your pillow, the next morning, the problem is gone.

I started to design for people like me, because we have different kinds of bodies, and it was difficult for me to find trendy clothes. So it was perfect! I was going to design for persons with Down syndrome.

But after a few months, everybody loved my clothes, so now, I am designing for everybody.

Now I work with three different groups of indigenous women from Guatemalan highlands, and they weave the beautiful materials I use for my designs.

Since London, I have been invited to travel to Rome, Miami, Mexico, Washington, and Panama, and I am booked for the rest of the year.

I am very, very happy. I have many projects and dreams, and I want the world to know that people with Down syndrome can dream and have goals. We can do it.

I had the opportunity to go to a regular school, to have all the stimulation I needed, and most of all I have a family that loves me dearly and believes in me.

When I was not accepted at the university, it was a NO, that I wanted to turn into a big YES!!!!!!!!

I love my life. I adore what I do, and I am willing to learn from "the university of life" and experience all I can.

I wish that every garment I so lovingly work on warms the dreams of other youngsters with different abilities to know that we can do it.

I believe we all together can knit a better world.

What marvelous strength to be told a blatant "no" and to do what she wanted anyway. Isabella knew what she wanted to do, and she does it. She does wonderful things every day. Not only does she do them every day, but she also does so much more than she had even thought of. It reaches far beyond the clothes and the fabric; she is inspiring and moving the world around her.

One of my favorite things about this story (there are many) is how Isabella and those around her, supporting her, are breaking down barriers. They are soldiers for a cause. While some may turn into advocates, speaking out for others to pursue their dreams, others become more silent soldiers. They simply stand strong, doing what they want to do, despite the naysayers, despite the barriers placed by misunderstanding, and despite any kind of troubles that naturally come. Anything worth doing is going to be difficult*.

*Side note: When things are easy, they actually tend to become more difficult. We don't grow or stretch like we would in hard times. We become complacent, which makes it harder when a change actually arrives, nor do we have skills to match the level required of us. For example, when I was a kid, I was obsessed with reading. Big surprise, right? There were things in my childhood that I wanted to block out and forget, which I did really well by escaping through books. I read so much that at one family gathering, we were all sitting around telling stories of things we had done, seen, or heard. I wanted to participate, but I had no stories. I had no experiences, and I realized I was living my life in neutral. It was easy, yes. However, it complicated things as simple as making conversation with my own family.

An example of these "silent soldiers" who simply live their lives despite obstacles and without becoming advocates is Vincent van Gogh. He was an artist, but he was not celebrated for his contributions until after his death. More is known about the personal life of van Gogh thanks to letters and correspondence with his brother, Theodore. Due to van Gogh's lack of success during his lifetime, he was supported by his brother. Not only was he not successful, but he also dealt with depression and other mental illnesses that had him labeled during his lifetime as a madman. This "failure" and "madman" still dedicated his life to his art, and he is now incredibly well known for his contributions to the artistic world and considered a genius.

This is not limited to the field of art. Take for another example Albert Einstein. He consistently received bad marks in school, particularly in math. Ironically, this is an area he excelled at later in life, creating formulas and discovering theories that were not only crucial to his day, but that are still being used today. Not only did Einstein struggle in school, but he was also considered autistic, and as a Jew, he was a refugee to America from Nazi Germany. Unlike van Gogh, Einstein was more of an advocate. He joined the NAACP to fight against racism, he was unapologetically himself, and he is quoted often with sayings that at the time were against the norm such as "I speak to everyone in the same way, whether he is the garbage man or the president of the university" and "If we knew what it was we were doing, it would not be called research, would it?"

Both of these men were different and unique. It was

these differences that led to their greatness. They are not alone; that list continues with names like Franklin Delano Roosevelt (who, despite being being partly paralyzed from a bout of polio, became president of the United States, the only one to serve three terms and who led the country through the brutal WWII), Harriet Tubman (a slave who led over three hundred others on the road to freedom), Wolfgang Amadeus Mozart (a musical genius who was also considered mad and is also rumored to have been autistic), Carrie Fisher (a famous actress and advocate for mental health), and Gandhi (who fought for the rights of his native India against the occupying Great Britain). Politics, music, art, science . . . the field itself does not matter. The leaders in these fields are always different. Even their differences are different. But it was their differences from the average that made them stand out and that helped others to see their genius.

Every human being has the capability for genius and greatness. It is up to us to develop it. When we are born, we have very few talents to speak of. We do the breathing thing really well. We manage crying and eating. Beyond that, we have curiosity. As we grow, we are constantly learning. We become more curious about some things than others. Everyone is interested in different things. Some are interested in fashion, others in sports, music, politics, theater, writing. The more we discover about the subjects that capture our interest, we gain understanding of them.

Understanding is the key to genius. The more we understand a topic thoroughly, inside out, backward, and examining every crevice, we can discover new things never seen by anyone else. We are able to see things no one else sees, and this allows us to do things no one else does. It doesn't matter how fast you find your genius. After all, the journey of a thousand miles begins with a single step. The important thing is the journey, not how fast we get there.

CONCLUSION

Healing Inspires Others

I CONFESS; sometimes it's hard to be writing all of this. I still have so much to work on myself. Life still sucks, and it's still hard. I feel a little bit like a hypocrite telling other people how to get past the rough stuff when sometimes I'm not even sure if I can do it myself. I think, though, that it might make it all the more real. I'm not immune to discouragement. I know it's hard. I struggle just as much as others. I'm continually learning more about how to overcome hard things as well.

Take, for example, the books I have written. I started out writing about my ability to cope with awkward things. So many of the things in my first book, *Awkwardly Strong: From Insecure to Inspirational*, are what helped me get to this point. So much in this book helps me with the awkwardness. That's the great thing about principles and ideas; they are flexible and interchangeable with varying situations.

I have seen these principles work for me, some better than others depending on the situation. Yes, they are interchangeable, but that doesn't make one the ultimate heal-all. Even reading about these things isn't the ultimate heal-all. True healing and growth will always take action on your part. Oftentimes, even then, we require help. The point is that you are worth healing.

Please don't overlook this part. People are so important on this path to healing. Whether it be a friend, a sibling, a significant other, a coworker, a cousin, a grandparent, or even a counselor or therapist. There are people who want to help you. When you open up to them, it is simply amazing what you can accomplish. I'm pretty sure I have used every one of those options I just listed, and I'm sure there are plenty others that didn't come to my mind. Whoever you thought of as you read this paragraph, let them know it. You don't have to do this on your own. Quite frankly, maybe they need you to open up so they can share with you, too. Someone has to start it.

Again, the only thing to be wary of is letting them tell you what to do. Other people are a great sounding board, but don't let them take away what is ultimately your decision. Some of the best advice I have ever received is advice is just that—advice. You are not required by some kind of contract to take that advice. You are the one who determines whether it will work for you or not. You decide if a confidant is giving good advice or bad. It may be good advice for them, and they've seen it work, but that does not mean it will work for you. Again, that is up to you.

Don't ever let anyone tell you what to think or how to feel. If you hurt, by all means, allow yourself to hurt. To be angry. To be grossed out. To be moved. To be happy. Especially to be happy.

You are the one in control of your own destiny. You are the one who makes the decisions. Sure, others can make choices regarding you, but you then get to choose if you follow or rebel, don't you? You have a choice. You may not always choose what happens to you, but you are the one who chooses how you react and the ultimate outcome. Isn't that a powerful thought? Look at how much power you hold. The power of your own life and to make of it what you will! It all comes back to the choices you make, especially in those low moments.

Do you realize how incredibly powerful you really are? How much ability you have to shape and craft your life, just like an artist, creating a stunning painting with some colored gloop? What a transformation. It will take work, just like painting does. Just like the artist, your soul becomes exposed to the masses, so it's not for the faint of heart. You do have that strength, though. Work that muscle, build that endurance. You are the strongest person you know. At least, you can be.

I never thought I would be as strong as I am now. That's saying something considering I still don't think I'm very strong. I still make stupid choices. I don't always take control of my life the way I should. Sometimes I hate making choices. But I'm better than I used to be. It's a process. I'm taking things one day at a time and one step at a time. And the journey has been absolutely breathtaking!

I had to hit rock bottom to get here. I didn't like where I was, and I had lost literally everything. It took a few months for me to finally look up at what was going on around me. I had to come to the realization that I wanted back in, back to experiencing life, not the travesty I was living. After that, to be honest, it probably took a few years with more highs and lows for me to look up higher at where I wanted to go. Then I had to work up the courage to start climbing. I still don't know why I let so much time pass. If I could do it again, the only thing I would change is that I would start sooner. Do it now. Look up. Start moving. Realize how strong you really are, and build on that!

That's really the key. You hit a low and then have to say, "Now what? Where do I go from here?" More importantly, "Where do I want to go and how do I get there?" Make your choice, then make your move!

Acknowledgements

LIFE CAN BE INCREDIBLY ROUGH, but it certainly helps to have a wonderful support system. I could not have had the experiences I had and survived without my amazing family. They lift me up in hard times and they encourage me in the ups and downs of writing. I can't express how wonderful they are in words (and I'm a writer, so that's saying something). So special thanks to Mom, Dad, Grandparents, and especially my siblings. They certainly don't realize just how much of an example they are to me and how much I need all of them. They are pretty great.

I also need to mention so many people who made this book as awesome as it is. It seriously takes a village for a book to happen. Great big thanks to Isabella Springmuhl for being willing to share her story with me and allowing me to share it with others. I love her passion for life, as well as her adorable clothes! She is an inspiration to me for overcoming the nay-sayers in her life.

Once again, Eschler Editing saved my life in taking a rough piece and making it shine. They are so great to work with and wonderfully professional services. Also had to stand by Megan Sawyer and her great work with the cover design. Then Fran Platt and Dayna Linton took the interior of the book to a whole new level. I wouldn't even dare hit publish without the level of professionalism these people bring to the table.

Also incredibly important to mention are the mentors who have helped and guided me along the way. Richie Norton and his daily inspirations, Benjamin P. Hardy and his marketing prowess, and Richard Paul Evans for sharing the ins and outs of everything writing. Each of these have taught me, and introduced me to so many amazing individuals that have just brought me to a higher plane. This tribe has taught me so much and I'm privileged to be a part of it.

Most importantly, you. It does no good to talk to an empty room, and without your support, there would not be a second book at all, much less any of the future ones I have planned. I am grateful to have you along on this journey with me. Thank you for giving me a reason to get out of bed in the morning and allowing me to live my dream.

About The Author

PAULA HAS ALWAYS BEEN in love with books even before she learned to read. Once she learned how, there was no turning back! She read so much growing up that she was once grounded from books for an entire summer during middle school. She has dreamed of being a writer as long as she can remember. She grew up in Logandale, NV, leaving her hometown to attend both Snow College and Brigham Young University-Hawaii to obtain a degree in International Cultural Studies with an emphasis in Communication.

Her senior year of high school, Paula started making noises. At 24, she was diagnosed with Tourette Syndrome. This has given her a unique perspective that she wanted to share with the world.

She currently resides in Salt Lake City, UT as an active blogger and writer. In addition to reading and writing, Paula loves singing and dancing in almost any genre. She loves being in and watching theatre productions, especially any musical performances. She is usually up for almost any activity, as long as it involves people. She enjoys all things island related and would love to travel the world. She is also actively involved in the Church of Jesus Christ of Latter Day Saints, serving both in her local ward and in the temple. Check out more info at mormon.org.

One More Note

THANK YOU SO MUCH FOR READING! I am ever so grateful to you. If you enjoyed reading this book, would you mind doing me a favor? Please share with your friends and leave a review. Reviews help others to find my work and helps me to grow so I can keep sending great content your way.

If you want to stay updated and in the loop, sign up for my free newsletter. Find the details by following me on Twitter, Instagram or Facebook—all @jesssqueaks. In fact, there is an additional gift for you when you sign up for the newsletter.